THE HUMAN COMPASS

Priscilla Mac

DEDICATION

To my Mother: this book is dedicated to all your love and support of my writing. Remember when my elementary school teacher called you in for a special conversation about me? I was in class looking at the two of you in the doorway thinking I was in major trouble. <u>When the teacher brought me over to the two of you,</u> she said, "Look at her pinky…. Mrs. McElveen, they are swollen and bleeding from writing. I just wanted you to know." You looked at the teacher without even looking at my hands and said, "Mmhmm. She'll be alright, just put a bandage on it." I was never taught to feel sorry for myself and didn't even know how. Thank you for being a strong part of my compass. Now you can say, "Well, she wrote a book so the bandage must have worked." I love you to the moon and back mommy a.k.a Sistah Jo.

To my wonderful readers, before you begin to turn the pages, I want you to understand that this is going to be a very direct book. It can be used to conquer mountains of hardships in your life. Wonder why so many folks are talented, rich, and educated, yet lose direction? It's because they didn't have a compass set up... properly. This is a true grit guide.

As my mother would say, "Life ain't no Soap Opera baby – you got to take the good with the bad and you can make it baby. You can make it!"

TABLE OF CONTENTS

INTRODUCTION

The Human compass consists of people in your life who are beneficial in certain areas.

At times, we can become frustrated with good people who are not responding to our needs for advice the way we'd like them to. This is NOT their fault; this is because you have not identified where they fit in your life.

Once you identify the people in your compass and where they stand, then you can activate it and begin to move in the right direction of your life much smoother.

So why do you need one of these?

Well, they say to surround yourself with people on the same mission as you. However, that quote has been taken out of its basic context.

I believe there to be many levels to that notion.

Yes, literally, people who are on the same mission.

The basic grid of North, South, East, and West is when most of the people in your life are collectively pursuing the same purpose.

CHAPTER 1

NORTH

North is the person who is your mentor in life. They are currently where you want to be. You can select someone who you know, but it's not too far-fetched an idea to select someone who you don't know personally, but yet admire. I have a mentor who I follow online. The beauty of Social Media is that you can connect more intimately with people receiving their advice, perspective, and ideas without being a pest. Your mentor should be someone who you take pride in modeling yourself after.

North is more likely to eventually affiliate with you if you are applying the advice and standards that they set out in life more than if you just want to be amongst them and in their circle of company. Remember, they are where they are for a reason, so they have seen ambitious mentees repeatedly and can smell the difference between an opportunist and an asset. A great mentor has accomplished the full potential of related areas that you desire to do.

So, how can you get even remotely close to these people? Well, if you have been applying their character and skills to your own life, then your results should mostly resemble theirs and it would be an evident connection. You should also have something to contribute to them.

I had a client who was set on being a future Billionaire. He had the ambition, the spark, the dream, and I feel like it's totally possible with his skills being in the stock market. I know that I have no knowledge of it and could use the opportunity to learn more. I felt like with that skill he certainly belonged among Billionaires. However, what he had in mind initially was the "no-no" that most people do. I thought that it would be great for him to seek one out and interview them. His idea was to ask questions, learn, and hopefully tag along side this person – that maybe they would see something in him and take to it.

Well, that's a no go. Always have something to GIVE. They see plenty of shiny faces, fast talkers, qualified on paper with a squeaky-clean track record day in and day out, screaming for attention with the belief that they have now made and deserve their attention.

WRONG!

This kind of personality is called a taker and people who have made it to the top dropped that kind of baggage long ago and so you wouldn't get past the "Contact Us" tab forum on their website with something like that.

In one of my favorite books, there is a story about a child being born who would change the world forever. There were three men who had heard about this child and wanted to be in his presence as an infant because they understood the miraculous connection. These men traveled afar, as the good book says.

First, let me stop right there and say, they aren't coming to you. You can absolutely meet them or with them and be a part of their lives, but remember, you are the mentee so you must reach out to them. They aren't going to call you out of the blue and they may not even be within miles of your city.

If you really want the good stuff that they have, you may have to travel afar to get it guaranteed.

They may be speaking hours away from you. Drive or catch the train! They may be doing a tour but not in your state. Book a ticket, hotel, and be there!

Getting back to the story, not only did they travel afar, they brought something called "Good tidings of great joy," not problems for him to solve. They didn't go there with the intention that because this individual has so much access and power that they can use it for themselves and gain a personal come-up by being seen with them. The heart was genuine. So, when you approach them and you want to be a part of their circle, instead of an average outside jo with problems that solutions are needed for, bring good tiding of great joy. Make sure that your motive is positive and that you are there for them.

Because they are considered your mentor, they are already giving you something as it is. You are benefiting from their words and literature that they have spent many nights sacrificing and going afar to collect the success that they have today. Can you see where you are already resembling them at this point?

What are these good tidings? How about the skills that they have? Not a business proposition or sales pitch, but a solution for some area in their life. The three men were called "Wise Men." They had brought Gold, Frankincense, and Myrrh – things that were not just of luxury, but of greater need at the time for the child. They knew ahead of time where this child was to be born – in a hay stack – so clearly, there were financial issues pending. That's why they brought the pure good stuff to him.

Do you know the needs of your mentor in order to provide reciprocity? Or are you sucking up all the good stuff from them? They brought their best – thee best. This family could use this to their advantage for a good amount of time. With the father being a carpenter, he can now run a successful business with these assets and provide a comfortable lifestyle and business to pass onto his son.

Bring something that is your best and you will be more than a mentee. This is a rewarding relationship.

Identify who your North is right now and write down their name. If you know them personally, make sure you have them on speed dial in your phone. Follow them on Social Media sites and connect with them for a meeting by inviting them out to a lunch or dinner that you will be paying for. Again, make sure you research them prior that you are bringing something to the table. Literally!

Here are a few questions to ask yourself:

+ What is my motive of being connected to this person?
+ Am I willing to apply advice given immediately?
+ Am I coachable?
+ Am I prepared?
+ Am I a good representation of them as a mentee right now?
+ Does this person bear fruit of what they do, meaning results?

Write out below who this person is and what you intend to do. What do they have going for themselves that you would like to replicate in your own life? Read their books and literature.

Work!

CHAPTER 2

SOUTH

South is the person who is always behind you to lift you up and make sure that you do not fall. They are your spiritual guidance. You need someone to keep you accountable and challenge you in areas of your faith – who is tried and true – who can handle any opposition you may give, because South is spiritual it's a sensitive situation.

This is outside of the workplace and surface things – this is internal dealings so be very careful who you receive guidance from in this area. Refrain from Spooky religious people who will get you way off track of your purpose and mission.

I am a believer in God and Jesus so my faith base is Christianity. However, I have had many run-ins with saints in church whom I thought I could look up to because of their titles and how many years they'd been in the ministry only to be disappointed that they didn't have the good sense that God gave them.

I shared with a woman a personal secret habit that I was trying to overcome. I went to the front of the church to be prayed over and everything. She was considered a prayer warrior ordained and the whole nine yards. This particular issue that I had required me to use something material in most cases. The following Sunday, she met me in the bathroom and apologized to me for saying something negative behind my back about what I had shared with her.

This was really her acting out the whole share-your-sins one to another and ask for forgiveness scripture to keep her conscious and her soul in good graces. I just said, "Oh, its ok," smiled, and hugged her. I knew she was a mess but then she went on further to say – and please BEWARE OF FOLKS LIKE THIS – are you ready? This is the famous one. She said, "The Holy Spirit told me that you need to stop using those things that you have and to get them out of your home." Because she had already embarrassed herself with the confession, I again hugged her, smiled, and said "Thank you so much sister, thank you."

Really, it was thanking you for showing me who you are. You just apologized for talking behind my back and now the frequencies between you and the Holy Spirit are apparently nonexistent. I never had any of the material that she spoke of to begin with and I never told her that I didn't which I'm glad, because that nonsense came straight from her mind. If it was really the Holy Spirit, it would have been a True statement.

The Holy Spirit knows what I have in my house, she was just guessing. Had I not been raised in the church to know better, something like that would have given me a bad perception of Christians – never to return again – with a chip on my shoulder. Fortunately, I have seen many like her in the house of the lord so it doesn't faze me. I just washed my hands literally in the sink and walked right on back to service. I still love and respect her dearly, but all I can say is… now I know.

You can identify good spiritual people because the information that they give you is Confirmation of what is already in your spirit, Not Fortune Telling the future for you. For a lot of church going people it can be your pastor, but you need someone more close and personal whose phone you can ring in the midnight hour. It does Not have to be a Pastor or even someone who attends your church. They just need to be solid and available. They need to be trustworthy. This has to be the most severe stable part of your Compass.

Your North isn't your South. Do not mix the two with shared weight like that. You want someone who you can be totally transparent with. Sometimes North will need to bear burdens with you. If you are consistent with this person, you will become in-sync, they can tell from your conversations if you are off track or not, and help get you back in line spiritually and mentally. They promote hope, prosperity and raw truth into your life. They confront areas of your life that need to be worked on within the conversations that you have because of their own walk and within those conversations without you even telling them everything they will begin to mention everything that you knew you needed to hear providing spiritual resolutions in alignment of your faith.

CHAPTER 3

EAST

East is your right-hand man or woman – the person who is there to love you. Let me say that may be all that they are there to do. They usually have characteristics of the entire Compass, but their priority and successful execution is to just love, so be mindful of that. I say this because I have many a time gotten my Compass mixed up with this one and become frustrated. I have asked my East for business advice, for spiritual answers, and for guidance.

Wrong!

I would get upset with their vain answers which really gave me nothing specific. Because I had chosen the head of a church itself, a prominent leader, you'd think this would be the Jackpot for spiritual, leadership, and business advice all in one bankroll. But that's just not their position in MY Compass. They are someone else's South and someone else's North. It's very important that you do not mistake all the gifts and talents of one person to belong to you. That being said, I observed this person's strong point in my life, which actually worked – and accepted it for what it was.

East is going to be on your side no matter what. Others may get tired of you at some point or unable to be there for you, but East provides unconditional love. They by example, not suggestion, are mentors so you will have to take what you can just from observation.

East is spiritual and everything, but again, you will get those things just from watching them. They are not to counsel you in those things because their personal walk is different from yours even though they have the same ultimate mission of greatness as you do.

My biggest mistake was placing too much on this person. I'd call them for every little piece of advice and sometimes they just did the best they could and gave me the wrong advice – not intentionally – but because they weren't an expert in that area.

Show gratitude to East by letting them know

how thankful you are to have them in your life. These kinds of people are often drained by people pulling everything from them, so don't be the extra one. Sometimes they will need you to listen to them as well. This is strictly a love relationship. Don't frustrate the situation or add stress by making it anything else.

East is strong enough to keep your most intimate secrets and will barely remember anything that you do wrong. They encourage you and always give affirmation, support, and are your biggest cheer leader. Look to East before you put yourself out there because they have your best intention at heart and want nothing more than the rest of the world to view you the same as they do. If ever that would possibly be any different, they would be the first to let you know.

East will take your happiness personally. Sometimes we make a move that we don't notice to be incorrect. I have to tell you this is your Social Media monitor for those who love to post. They are the true Brand Consultants without any certification. Just heart.

I have made emotional statuses on my Facebook page and would receive a phone call from my

East to take it down. This is because they knew the intention of my brand and future and will protect it.

A lot of people could use an East. I'm sure you can tell who doesn't have one. They will get on Social Media and cuss the world out only the next day to post how grateful to God they are. Or the half-naked club photos followed by a photo of their children.

Or the subliminal. You know what? The subliminal are super bad. These are posts that people who are bleeding make, so that someone else can see it and feel it in some kind of way.

Yes, a post on Social Media where millions can see, for one person to supposedly get a clue.

Craziness!

I can confess that my marriage has been in deep shambles, but you will never see a post displaying that. It's not even being transparent, because 90 percent don't care and the remainder are glad that it's you.

These people have not identified their East. They need someone to talk to who loves them and who they can trust so they don't pull a dear diary on the world and make a fool of themselves.

This happens from all education levels, races, and economic classes. You will be surprised how someone with an education will get on Social Media and act like a plum fool. It's actually discouraging. If this is you, then continue to read so that you may get your Compass together.

CHAPTER 4

WEST

Ahhh! The great and powerful West. What I love about West is that they never ever change. This is the most stable of them all going forward with physical effective instant results.

West is your LOGIC individual. They are solely logic. I refer to them as the SPAC of your Star Trek voyage. There is no emotion here – only fact, mission, and execution.

How do you identify this person?

West has what I call a case of the "I can't help its" and has been this way their entire lives. They live by structured rules that they never ever compromise.

That being said, you can assure yourself that they will not bend their rules for you. This is the Vice-President of company you. They have your mission as a focus, not your feelings.

Remember, this is what your East is for, so if you

confuse the two, your feelings will be hurt.

I have made the mistake of venting to West for consolidation only to receive a step-by-step plan to continue with my life. They won't cry with you and they have high expectations. The only way they will even fool with you outside of advice is if they have seen a non-risk to do so.

Remember, West can't help being calculative, and will apply this nonverbally even in the notion of working with you. They are very upfront and to-the-point honest people. If West decides to get in the fire with you, be grateful because you have passed a thousand tests that they have observed at a distance before going through this process.

To have a West is to be legit. They keep you focused when you wonder off into la-la land from listening to so many motivational speeches. They not per say poke your balloon, but they make sure you understand that we visit the mountain top but we live on ground.

West will briefly celebrate every achievement that you make and execute before giving you another task and hill to climb with a straight face.

They compartmentalize your ideas, give you a realistic way to approach them, and from there it's your job to execute. They absolutely will not do it for you and make themselves clear about it.

If you are a sensitive person like me, brace yourself for the break in this relationship, because there will come a time when I guarantee that you will want to cut West off because of how direct they are. It's not that they are trying to be malicious at all or even rude but the fact base can be difficult to handle and at times super strong.

I have once vowed never to speak to my West again. They hurt my feelings so bad. I had shared a business plan with them that I thought to be so amazing. I had everything lined up, and even thought I had answers to every possible opposition they would have given me.... except the truth.

I believed in my goal and plan but they told me, in all honesty, how, why, and the experience that they've encountered of others as to why it wouldn't work. They had much resource and I couldn't fight it.

I felt like this person was against me and didn't believe in myself. Beware of these emotions because you can lose really good people on your team by thinking that folks are against you. Carefully consider their input. It doesn't have to be the final say but it should have priority impact – if not then, you have a weak Compass to begin with.

You must sure-fire trust these folks more than your impulsiveness. As a good book says, "To thine own self be true."

When you come to a crossroads of whether you should take West's advice or muster up the courage to just do it anyway, open up your files of past experiences, and examine how well that behavior has worked out for you. If the result is good, proceed with caution. If you find that you're famous for falling flat on your face, humble yourself, bite your tongue, and adhere to the value given with gratitude and grace.

West will build your mental and emotional muscles. Once they are through with you, haters will be like little flies. The reason people crumble and break when they become popular and find out that everybody doesn't like them is because they never had a West to give them a bite for their own good. They think that everyone is going to accept their great ideas and notions and that's just not the way the real world works.

West will prepare you for the way the real world is going to perceive and respond to you, so consider them a confidence course of life.

There is nothing someone on the job can say about my work in criticism form that I have not experienced the emotional wave of behind the scenes with my West and no one can rip a behind like my West so others are child's play. That's how strong they will make you.

I have worked with a woman who corrected me constantly because she was afraid that if higher up did so that it would crush my spirit. Oh, no, honey – I am a big girl – I can take a mighty blow – you have no idea how many times I've had my head chopped off and had to sew it back on because I wear pearls around my neck to hide the scars and all you can see is beauty.

Make no mistake that West loves you and even has respect and admiration for you which is why they are a willing to be part of your team. But this is how their brain operates:

- Focus
- Mission
- Complete
- Execute
- Time Management
- Details

THIS IS IT!!!!

Expect nothing else and anything extra is a pure privilege. A lot of times, more than they should be, subordinates – if allowed to be a part of a superior's life – will become too comfortable with them and behave as a peer when its working time.

Fear not, West will not have this out of you. They maintain the focus when it's focus and fun, if any, when it's fun.

You will not be able to throw smoke screens or come up short on anything less than what you set out to do. West will call you out on it right away, locking eye to eye contact while doing so, and cut down any excuse given with a hattori hanzo of steel sword.

Don't ever lie or try to avoid West because of how they are. Facing this confrontational personality head-on will strengthen you.

Why?

Because West knows who they are. They have been themselves their entire lives and folks who said they wanted advice from them have run from them.

Wests have very few friends but to have someone who can stand their storm and face the flack brings a great respect. They are your personal Drill Sergeant preparing you for battle to hit the target every time and they want to see you win.

After a few weeks of not speaking to my West, I apologized and mended the relationship. This made them aware of my peak and even with an ambitious spirit, how humble I can be, which means my destination is important and rather urgent. It can be the most uncomfortable relationship of all. But I knew I needed their truth, and they were absolutely right.

That business plan would have been the worst mistake of my life and I would have wasted much valuable time pursuing it just to get to a certain place that had nothing to do with my purpose. With a mind of a high order, I thought my plan would have been a clever way to gain instant income and my then version of success. However, when I listened to West and let go of the older version, new opportunities arrived.

Now the mending of our relationship wasn't for us to continue with an understanding that there is only so much that I can take. The mending was an understanding that I am now mature enough to take on this relationship come what may.

You never want West to begin watering down things for you or you will miss the fruit and treasure of having them in your life. Instead, you will have to put your big girl/boy draws on and carry on. In other words, now I am brave and ready to continue on with the mission – you won't have any more emotional spasms out of me. A long apology was unnecessary because Wests are usually beyond the fluff and ready to just get back on course.

If you haven't noticed by now that the writing in this particular chapter is repetitive, but takes different angles, then do so. The reason, again, is because this personality is repetitive. You want a non-wavering person who cannot help but be this way.

Unlike North, you will have nothing to offer West that they will accept anyway because to them, it's not the Focus of the relationship and they'd rather just keep it to the point of your mission. Charm and compliments will be brushed off instantly after giving. Nevertheless, still do so just because of who you are. In essence, you should hold West to the highest regard of your Compass out of all the directions.

People often hold North to their highest regards. One day you will outgrow your current Compass but not West. You may get bigger than North and you may have to become, at some point, a confidant to East as the relationship is of shared emotions and we can't put South on too much of a spiritual pedestal because we are all human.

Don't be surprised if North falls at some point in their lives. But West was never there to impress you, console you or for you to immolate their lives so this one has no reason to change whatsoever.

Can you identify your West?

Who is the person who tells you the honest truth, whether you like them or not? Be honest with yourself. You will need to reach out to them on a weekly basis with updates and prove that you want to build a relationship with them involving your new resolution of growth. Just start by sharing with them your actual intention, don't ask them for any help. They know when to help you and a phone call is not going to get it.

To West, you will look like someone seeking a hand out. Just keep up with them weekly letting them know about what you're working on and they will naturally begin to give you advice. They won't let you into their lives to give them advice so don't think that this is about to be a trade of information. Once again, they will immediately divert the conversation back to your mission to keep you focused because these people fix things on their own by reading books like this and they have a way of getting through that doesn't involve your advice.

Wests are perfectly fine with giving to you without receiving anything at all in return. Their success is already manifested so mainly just be humble, listen, and be ready to do the work.

If West gives you an assignment and you do not complete it and return to them with an excuse, they will ignore you. They don't want you to contaminate their life with your slacking. They will get back to you at a later time, when you are ready to be serious with risks figured out ahead of time or at least identified.

West will be your blessing, but they are not here to play games with you, so tuck your shirt in and pull your pants up with these ones!

Write out a list of people who you think are eligible to be your West. Here are the traits necessary:

+ They must have experience in accomplishing what they set out to do.
+ They must be hard core perseverance.
+ They hardly see any opposition because they always find a way to make it work.
+ They do not attach their emotions to goals.
+ They are direct, clear communicators and straightforward.
+ They love you dearly and want your success for you, it should go without even saying.

- ✦ They maintain control in crisis situations.
- ✦ They are usually not on Social Media Platforms they can't stand it.

When you find this g cherish it.

CHAPTER 5

NORTH EAST

Now that we have laid down the basic Compass which applies to your life and character, the main core people who are going to hold you together shall enter into the next level.

Have you ever heard the term, "There are levels to this?" There are definitely levels. The next one is catered specifically to your goal, not YOU. Remember that the basic Compass is about you, this is NOT. This is directly about your goal.

For example, if you are a book-writer, then the basic Compass will be the people who adjust your mindset to do so, but going forth, you will need people who are actual authors.

Remember: there is only ONE North, the rest is outsourcing.

Your North East needs to be someone you can be in physical contact with for mentoring – who will provide you with hands on training (physically doing the work assignments.) They should be affiliated with your dream because they have accomplished a magnitude of it themselves. The difference with North East is that I can call my East on the phone and fully vent about life to the point where I can say things that I really shouldn't say without being embarrassed.

It's OK to be transparent with North East, but don't get too loose with your business because the person will change. As you evolve and move to different locations, the position remains. The person fills in the spot changes. You don't want too many ears receiving too much of your business. As a writer, I would vent to them about writing blocks and situations specifically in that area. Keep it cute honey.

I don't know why I even wrote that. I guess because it's my book. But going forward, make sure you utilize North East on a regular basis. They keep you in touch with your emotions, which exploits the creativity in your endeavors. They nourish your dream with acclamations. It's so awesome because you know it's true coming from those who have done it.

North East will have the same glimmer in their eye as you do when you connect about your direction. You should feel comfortable with sharing some personal things because they will tell you how to deal with it on their level.

If I am a writer and having personal issues in my household, I would share the generic version of it with North East. Trust me – they understand and are not trying to be your BFF. But they can share their equally generic testimony with you of how they got through that situation as well.

The case may be that you: have no money for a sitter. You need peace and time to write your book, but you're stressed over bills that you can't pay. Your self-esteem is low and your health is jacked.

You can say this to East but to North East: "I'm really going through a lot right now with kids and home life. I'm just trying to get on my feet to finish this." They hear you and can respond. "I wrote my first book during a divorce – it was a big deal for me…." There they go spilling the beans for you to make a soup of encouragement with. Eat up the Yummy. It's a healthy relationship for you.

NOTE: Beware that North East is a temporary position. With your main Compass operating, there may come a time when you pass them up in life, so be mindful how much you do tell according to the length of your relationship.

There are never enough years from zero to a thousand for anyone except the main Compass to have too much information about you. I don't care what they share you. Nobody, I repeat nobody, gets in but the MAIN COMPASS. Capiche'.

Write out the candidates in mind that you have. There can only be one for this position. Pick the one that resembles the strongest of the following qualities.

+ They are currently successful in your area of purpose and expertise.
+ They share the same lifestyle you do: children/no children, perfectly maybe their kids are older than yours so that they have the experience of starting out with little ones. Or they may be a person who shares

the same void of not being able to have children since your age range.

+ They have the completion of what you want in life.

+ They should be several steps ahead of you.

+ You can identify and research their work digitally and study it. There should be footprints and cookie trails that this person has left already in this life.

You are not looking for a rising person; you are looking for a person at the summit.

North East has the key to your true North so work with them closely and tweak all errors to get them right. You want to Impress this person. Because they are a North East, they will most likely immediately work with you once they see the fruits of your labor. This puts you into the big leagues so make sure you execute accordingly. They will eventually want to be a part of your skills and allow you into their world of confidential information.

Let nothing that they tell you about them personally deter you in any way about the magnitude of their capabilities. You will see

35

flaws, but keep your eyes on their gifts and talents and be grateful, if at all, they do become comfortable enough to trust you with anything else.

Be trust worthy with this individual. Norths have Power, never forget that. Their network is massive. In the instant that you cross one, for whatever reason, your entire operation could be wiped out with one phone call gone national so in other words:

Don't take their kindness for weakness.

Write out who your North East is here:

_____

_____

_____

_____

_____

_____

_____

_____

CHAPTER 6
NORTH WEST

The wonderful North West. I must tell you this is going to be the person who challenges you in your specific industry. They will get on your very last nerve because they require perfection and attention to every little detail. You will never get it right with them and they will criticize everything that you do and what's worse, they will always be right. You will need the following with these people.

✦ Vitamin B12 stress supplements. Take two at a time.

✦ Create a motivational music and speaking playlist to listen to every single day to keep your self-esteem intact.

✦ The power of deep breaths.

✦ Prayer and have South pray as well.

✦ A collection of bible scriptures.

✦ Between 6 to 8 hours of sleep or you will snap... trust me.

Again, North West will change as you grow further along, but each will be equally necessary. Up the anti of the original East because you are with them every day, most likely working with them.

I can't tell you how many times my eyes have rolled into the back of my head dealing with my North West. My God, I can never get any slack or anything right. They always want more from me than they expect from others and I found that to be so unfair.

I volunteered at a Media Broadcasting company and the person who had brought me into it had me feeling grateful to be there in the beginning. I came in regular hours 9:00 a.m. to 12:00 p.m. which was good for a while until my life circumstances began to cause a problem with me being on time. Being five minutes or even three minutes late was a no-no. I literally walked in three minutes late and was yelled at in a room full of people that if it ever happened again, I would completely be removed from the program.

So, guess who suddenly had an epiphany about being punctual? That's right. I had to make it on time no matter what.

I was then given a more excruciating schedule to arrive at three a.m. in the morning. My thing was, I am not getting paid to be here and my expectations are increasing. I was told to arrive to work prior to set up while the people who worked there showed up at a comfortable 9:00 a.m. empty-handed every single day.

Everything that I edited and wrote was in much need of surgery, but the people who worked there turned in soup sandwich on a weekly basis. My on-camera performances were always scrutinized with different implementations and sometimes even deleted when others wouldn't even stand in front of the camera.

I was dismissed at every pitch to be actually hired. I was constantly told that I wasn't ready. Meaning not good enough. I couldn't do one thing and when I did that thing, it needed work. Then there was something else that I needed to do. When I did those, they needed work. Then there were a chunk of things missing. When I did those, the timing took too long. When the timing was good, there were misspelled words. When there weren't misspelled words, there were words used wrong. When there weren't words used wrong, there were details that needed to be researched. When the details were researched, there was a problem with the outsource of research used. When there wasn't a problem with the outsource of research used, there was not enough enthusiasm in another area all the way until they went home for the day.

That's when there was peace in the office space and I got the chance to learn what they had taught me at my own pace, without criticism directly on my neck and making corrections instead of allowing me to do so. I never once complained in front of this individual because one thing I knew for sure was that perfection was their personality.

Does it matter whether or not their motives were for or against me? No. It only matters how I used their motives.

Now that we are dealing with a North West, not a regular West, let me make myself clear. North West doesn't have to care about you at all. They don't have to like you and they may even be your enemy. They could very well be totally working against you.

I must say that those are the golden best North Wests that you will ever have. They are the REAL WORLD your original West has been preparing you for. They will tear your purpose apart by the minute relentlessly and slay your spirit. Sometimes they don't even know they are doing this. They just want perfection and you being in the hot seat as the student makes them come across as being a pest along the way. You want me to be completely honest with you?

You will never make it in life until you get one of these North Wests and conquer weaknesses that they freely point out. You will have many. You must NOT SNAP. You must humble yourself and bite your tongue, look straight ahead and do whatever it takes. Take all the good from it.

Am I mad that I'm on a strict schedule, and someone else gets to show up when they want to? Yes, but it makes me a punctual person so I'm not losing anything.

Am I mad that I take my time to wake up at 1:50 a.m. to get my makeup and hair done to be on time at 3:00 a.m., when others who are employed there may not do the same? Yes, but now I am the woman who shows up on time in full gear at the crack of dawn without a hint of tiredness and ready to take on the spot action.

Am I mad that I have to show up beyond prepared every day, while others could care less about their work? Yes, but it gave me the experience of my field of work.

Am I mad that my presentation has to look like Albert Einstein put it together, while others spin around in their chairs with nothing to show for the day and a third grade paragraph called a story? Yes, but it taught me to be tight in my work.

All of the above are venting thoughts when you go through this process and begin to compare yourself to others. This is a boobie trap because in reality, I had no clue what other employees' responsibilities were, yet you see how the mind can take you on a bitter trip. Be careful of that, and remember you have flaws, too. Comparison and bitterness cause you to exaggerate. I didn't even show up like that on a daily basis and there were times in the beginning especially, when I had trouble showing up on time with my new schedule. Fatigue is very serious in this area so take notes in a journal about your perception of things when the heat turns up on you like this.

North West is always working for you whether they realize it or not. They are ensuring that you are super perfect – that there are no crumbs that anyone, not even themselves, can catch. If you're really pissed at them for the way they went about it once you understand their motive, be highly better than them, pass them up in the industry, and behold you'll get a new one.

You can't run from these folks. And no, you can't strangle them. Their purpose in your Compass is to make sure that your purpose is executed flawlessly. If at all, they are a companion of any kind, be grateful.

I was fortunate enough to have a Northwest that I still to this day am thankful for as a real friend, not a Yes Man just because she knew and liked me and made herself clear about professional boundaries.

Always let them know that you appreciate the time that they are putting into you. Recognize their accomplishments, as they do need to have accomplishments, in order to be a part of your

Compass.

North West is always about doing better and they can take constructive educated criticism that makes sense. Note that they still have the emotionless Spak from Star Trek characteristics, so they are not in tune with how they may come across to people and the moments that they are pleasant are sure to be genuine with love. They are very good at leadership, but the people on higher levels that they need access to don't always see it right away, so they find themselves looking through glass ceilings very often. These are hardworking people who are very thorough so if you become a leader yourself make sure that you have one of them on your team and learn from them.

In conclusion, eat up all that you can from North West's work performance. Observe their personality, how people take to them, and make adjustments to yourself.

Who is your North West?

North West is the person who is where you want to be that will take you to perfection but only through a severely bumpy road. You don't want to reach your destination easily because, as the saying goes, "Easy come… Easy go."

Appreciate and find the value in North West. In the long run, you may very well be the only real friend they have. But, initially it's not about friends. Stay focused with this person.

Remember, West stays focused for you, but YOU Must govern yourself accordingly and carefully to stay focused with North West. On this level, you are too close. This is the door that when people get rejected from they often give up, go off, and call it quits. That's what they want you to do because there is no room for quitters on the other side of the door.

You wouldn't even make it to Success, unless you can put up with some estranged people who do the darndest things for reasons we will never know about.

You have to become Rock Solid with North West, so when they throw rocks at you, those things will just bounce off and fall straight to the ground.

If anything, North West will just be getting some arm exercise in. Trust me – once you become suited up and unstoppable, their arms will get tired of throwing those rocks at you. So, outlast the situation.

CHAPTER 7

SOUTH EAST

If you have caught on by now the way that the Compass is working, then you know that South East is the spiritual person who loves you. South East is on the second level grid, catered particularly to your purpose. They work in the same field as you do.

Everyone who shares the same profession as you do does not share the same faith as you do, so South East is a person who does share your faith and edifies you as well within the realms of work. I just have to touch on these things because the Christian community is by far the largest, so it's most possible that they get more confused than any other.

South East is not the person to be laying hands and anointing oil on you at the office. You should still maintain a professional attitude and not take shared faith for granted or assume that South East is supposed to pull more strings than you qualify for because you both believe in God.

There is no sense in turning South East into a demon and fasting them down as some sort of spirit whenever you don't get your way. There is nothing more embarrassing to the Christian community than a lazy Christian who likes to come to work late, leave early, put in 70 percent effort, play loud gospel music, and claim the favor of God over their lives.

What kind of God do you serve that can't even get you to complete your work with enthusiasm for the day? Don't be the person on the job that's sharing scriptures with everyone and oh so much wisdom, but you aren't leading by the accomplishments of being thorough with your work. That preaches about who your God is more than your mouth.

I met a man in the lobby of another Media Broadcasting department that I worked for. My client was actually one of the on-air personalities there, but his show wasn't so much religious. He was still trying to find his way with God as well, so having guests to come on and speak about it was a great idea, not only for the audience listening, but for him as well.

One night after a successful show, we were packing up our belongings to leave and an elderly man came in the door. He said he was just checking the place out and that he was soon to be on air himself. "Oh, that's wonderful!" I said. He then began to share with us how all of this was meant to be and what God had told him. He began sharing scriptures of what God said in the bible. About the longest ten minutes ever went by and then I realized by experience that this was a "Spooky."

Remember what we talked about in the South Chapter? Beware of the Spooky ones.

I tried to give this man a hint by walking over to the wall and snatching my laptop cord out of the wall, implying we are shutting down. He thought that my client and I were a married couple so he looked at him and asked, "Oh, and is this your wife?" My client said no and I can bet you a thousand dollars if he would have said yes, the man would have said the Holy Spirit told him so. Oh, you don't believe me? When my client said, "No, this is my Publicist," you know what the man said? God has told me to write a book. I knew it was the reason that we met today. This is all his plan. The word of God says...... and on he went.

See, I don't quote aloud what the word says, I just do it. And it does say to test the spirit so that's exactly what I did. I looked him square in the eye and said, "Have you started your book?"

"No," he said.

"Oh, OK, do you have a title? What is it about?"

Be careful giving these folks a stage to stand on with questions because this man took center stage. I could hear the violins playing in the background he was so good. I'm telling you, this man looked into the air with tears in his eyes, voice cracking, and spoke to us personal information about his father and what happened to him.

Now, we just met you so for this to be shared is not at all about God, this is a personality flaw. I said, "Well, I have an editor. When do you want to get started?"

The man replied, "Uh, well really soon."

I pulled out my calendar and said, "Sir, I need a date and time. If you already have the content, then it can be published."

The man said, "Well it's not completely written yet. I want to see where the lord is leading me with it and all."

I said, "OK, well I also assist in the planning process so we can set a schedule of time and dates for you to work on your book all the way up to completion and have it published on a goal date. When do you want to get started sir?"

"Uh, well I'm not even sure if I really want to write…".

No more to be said, I looked at my client. "You ready to go?"

"Yeah let me turn out the lights and lock the door."

Now my client and I had some important things that we needed to discuss privately, so I looked at the man and said "It was nice meeting you sir. We are getting ready to get out of here you take care."

Not getting the hint, the man said. "Uh yes ma'am, I'm just going to walk out here with ya'll since you're headed this way".

Do you know he talked to us about Peter in the bible and a number of other characters all the way out of the door and to my car? We were standing outside so long that I pretended to have lost my keys upstairs in the office so that my client and I would have to leave him and go back inside so the man could go on home, but my client didn't catch on and said, "Oh I don't have any way to get back into the office."

"Ah, I found them." I said… never mind.

Dear Lord, "What kind of spirit is this?" I thought to myself. I knew he meant well but something was just not right about him and his delivery of the gospel.

What's worse is that my client is not one who grew up in the church so this was a rather poor example and discouragement of spiritual advising to any degree. Things like this just make people say that Christians are ridiculous and crazy.

Please do not judge us all by the "Spookies." Most of them attend churches which teach that behavior or they may have a mental disadvantage. They only comprehend the spiritual aspect and are mentally unavailable to communicate in English Earth language.

Make sure your South East has a good head on their shoulders or you will catch the contagious "Spooky" disease.

I met a person who trusted someone to be their South East because she was an older woman and supposedly full of wisdom. She knew the scriptures in and out along with wise sayings and is one of those who can see things in dreams and prophecy but her house looked like a filthy pig sty on the outside that the humane society needed to eradicate from the property. And the woman didn't keep up with her own appearance.

I would never want to even know what the inside of that house looked like. From the outside, it looked like it stank. Even Joyce Meyers says, "Some people are out trying to cast out devils and they don't even have authority over a sink full of dirty dishes yet."

I saw a girl outside across the street smoking a blunt and talking to a pimp. Guess what, though? Her lawn and yard was in tip top shape. Why do people who aren't even living right have better sense than you do to pick trash up off the floor, but you want to prophecy over my life. No way!

If you mess around with halfway people like that, you will be a half way result.

Who is in your spiritual corner that is well rounded? Someone that you can talk to? Someone qualified to talk to?

Write your selections below.

_____

_____

_____

_____

_____

_____

_____

_____

_____

_____

_____

CHAPTER 8

SOUTH WEST

South West is your stern and firm spiritual person within your particular profession. Remember, WEST does not have to share the same faith as you do. However, South West does. They are there to hold you spiritually accountable. They keep your integrity intact, but they are not as raw and edge cutting as the basic West.

South West will most likely not come to you and tell you what to do with your life hardly all, though they can see from a distance. You will have to approach them and ask for direction and feedback.

Be prepared to receive some truths and clarity outside of emotions. Sometimes we have an emotional epiphany that makes us think that we are ready to take on something. It's not that we aren't, but the emotion in the epiphany portion is such a high and good feeling of cleanliness and redemption that once the hard part, labor and dirty work are placed in front of us as a snap into reality of what it actually takes to manifest our desires, we become – let's just say it – lazy.

We procrastinate and come up with excuses as to why no longer 'now is the time.' Do you know what people will actually say? Here is another sad one… "I'm waiting to see what God says."

Let me faint for a second.

Every time I hear this, I believe the person saying it thinks they are in the times of Abraham, Noah, and Moses.

Honey, God is not building anymore Arks so that kind of waiting on the voice is just pure procrastination. Please don't use God as an excuse to do so when you can clearly read the bible and figure out what He has to say along with options for your life right away. You can even more so take into account the simple fact that you desire a thing. Your desires come from God and it's your passion. So, yes,

"Go forth with whatever it is and allow the bible and people placed in your life to guide you across treacherous water that you wouldn't be able to get yourself across." Les Brown.

I had a South West who gave me assignments to do. Some of them were so profound and life changing that I did not complete them. I was astonished at what they were, how they even came about, and afraid to fail at making that kind of change at the time. I wasn't ready.

When I approached the South West for this particular position of accountability, what I had in mind was nothing major – just slight work to check in here and there – like have her email me or text me a few scriptures to read weekly. Then we would pray together. You can see where she would be doing most of the work.

In this scenario, you are turning someone into your spiritual slave to do all the work for you. And some people will actually take something like that on if they don't have the sense that God gave them. If she were to do that, it would have crippled and made me spiritually handicapped to constantly seek her relationship with God as more valuable and credible than my own.

A true spiritual leader and/or mentor creates leaders, not followers. What the South West would be doing is confirming and adding logic value to my faith-walk with God and how I approach my profession as a believer – not putting a bottle in my mouth every time I cry.

There has to be a level of maturity in order to receive a South West. Make up in your mind that you are capable of taking on this relationship and providing the results necessary in your life. I can assure this would be very beneficial in the long run. The situation could be quite an uncomfortable experience. The worst thing you can do when you are involved with a South West who is stretching you to grow, is become upset with them and complain about them to other people so that they can help you fool yourself.

We sure know how to tell a side of a story and paint a certain picture, but in reality "All that they say about you isn't a lie."

I believe that people often create imaginary haters to deflect their own foolishness. In most cases, they drag groups of people along with them to confirm their nonsense behavior as right. This is where the South West is at risk with YOU.

I know we all like to believe ourselves to be the victim and have to pray about how others mistreat us, hoping that God could just remove them from our lives or change their hearts. We never take time to cover the tracks of who we are a burden to.

Who is praying at night about you and your attitude because something you said has scarred them for life and left them with a low self-esteem? Who have you given such a hard time to?

A South West has to deal with your attitude when they tell you the truth and risk how you handle it. I have witnessed prestigious educated people in the church spread vicious rumors about a person just because they didn't like what and how something was said to them. But, when they shared the story with others, they made sure that it was in a way that they were a victim and the other person should just be ashamed of themselves.

People follow up behind foolishness I can tell you that right now. My mother says, "You want to know the truth about a lie? Somebody will believe it and Somebody wants to believe it."

Make yourself a humble and trustworthy student. If you do, you will get a lot out of this relationship. You don't want them to hold back or only deal with you because it's the Christian thing to do. They should feel comfortable enough to know that you are a big boy/girl enough to handle and tackle what comes your way.

If you do need a little affirmation and love, then share what you're doing with South East. They would love to congratulate, empower, and console what South West is setting out for you to do and will even keep that relationship encouraged.

This is why it is important to understand the roles of people in our lives and utilize them properly.

CHAPTER 9
THE GEOGRAPHICAL VIEW

While your orbit is moving you into the right direction of your purpose in life, you have all of these people watching you and making sure that things are intact. They are your Super Hero team – the Marvels come to life, if you will. But who is watching them? Can you trust them?

Surely, we know that people are only human beings. How many times have we seen a Judas come forth for 30 pieces of Silver each and every time?

Here is the truth: very few people will be loyal and 100 percent trustworthy. The only one you can trust is God.

There will be times when you can't even trust your own instincts, I assure you that. My mother told me repeatedly since I was a child, "The only thing for certain is Jesus, so you had better know him for yourself, child."

Each individual is a participant of your team.

With that being said, let's look at things from a Geographical View or as I like to call it the eyes of God. The most brilliant of them throughout time and history – liked or disliked – believed or unbelieved – has been tried and proved true.

I love to study the brain of God. There are so many parallels to it, you can never get enough and each dimension grows with meaning.

For a moment, in order to understand the mind of God, try thinking like Him. Emerge in his cause so you truly get how this Compass works.

Without taboo, let's say that you are God and you have a mission. What would you do? You would create people and place different talents and abilities in them that they are born with.

For the example of the Compass, let's say you made Sarah to be a vocal ambassador to get the word out and reach a mass number of people on behalf of your mission. You would input certain skills into Sarah such as speech, Law of Attraction, and the ability to comprehend. These are the basic tools that need to evolve in a major way.

Now Sarah herself is no gem of a character. She

has major flaws, including a nasty attitude, and is always getting into trouble by being disobedient and so forth. But it's NOT about Sarah. This girl has your Billion-dollar investment inside of her so the last thing you're going to do is shut down the operation because of her flaws. Since you are a master Creator from up high, you have an enormous amount of creations to put into place which will shape her life right on up, but yes, it will take time.

Keep in mind that you have an enemy who wants you and your creations to become a laughing stock and fail at the good so he works against you by providing Sarah with everything she needs to fail. He, too, has people who will come into her life. The more of these people he destroys, the more likely your precious Sarah, although born for your purpose and with your Billion dollars, she is born into the very home and or environment that he has built reputation of and created.

Therefore, it very difficult for Sarah to realize her worth. He uses Jean, one of his teaching creations, to come into her life in the school house. There she encourages, uplifts, and validates Sarah.

Now Sarah has an inkling of herself, but that's not enough. She has nasty habits nurtured by the enemy to break her worth. He ignites desires in her and she realizes that she cannot achieve them with her nasty habits. These are only seeds.

Getting to the Compass, He creates each individual with a special gift that is an asset to the mission he has set for you. It's not about you and it's not about them.

We are all Humans following a much larger Compass. We are all a part of something bigger than we can even fathom.

This example book is so small that it's broken down into the smallest form of the larger Compass just to cater to You. You, as well, are a North, South, East, or West for someone else.

We discussed in the beginning the importance of being surrounded by people on the same mission as you because this circulation keeps what God has going forward. I have had people be a part of my Compass for all of five minutes before their integrity was compromised and turned against me, but the bulk of their purpose remained and worked in my favor. God had given me their five minutes of fame and when they attempted to pull the rug out from underneath my feet, I had too much weight for it to be moved.

Be not surprised by people who grin, hug you, kiss you, ask about your children, help you at your lowest points, cry with you yet will put a bullet of jealousy right between your eyeballs when you least expect it. These can be short term friendships, but some people are unaware that even a friend of 100 years, a parent, or a sibling is capable – just because they are people.

There are some things you better not tell anybody but God. Meanwhile, you have to be strong enough to let people in, take the risk of a licking, and enjoy the positive fruits being bared at the same time.

The best thing to do is separate the man from the gift. You will have to look at them with Logic, Love them, use your spiritual wisdom and discernment, and keep your eyes on the target that you want to hit. Continue to keep going North.

God has created this Compass so he will make

all and any adjustments necessary. Build a relationship with God by getting to know how he operates in relationships. You can do this by reading the bible and noticing how situations play out. Then you will be able to identify the same for yourself and notice similar patterns.

I met a woman who I clicked with really well. Our personalities were similar and we had the same family goals. I confided in her and we were together all the time – her children and my children. When things got super bad for me, she was there for me and my family. She cried, hugged me, and saved me from devastation that would have taken years, if ever, to recover from. I thought we would be best friends forever.

I even thought this relationship was God-given. She was a woman of faith with a religious education background and seemed to be encouraging. I was grateful for her help, but I am one to quickly get on my feet and surpass expectations. This is where things got ugly.

Here is a side note. Beware of people who want you to be beholding to them. She was under the impression that because of what was occurring in my life, she was to be my lifetime rescuer, and

I was some kind of pet of hers to constantly say, "It's OK," and reveal her glory of building a person back together. This type of situation makes some people feel good and worthwhile because they are able to restore the other, but some take it to the extreme.

I no longer needed tissues to sob into. I had moved on to bigger and better things. She wasn't even wise enough to research my lifestyle before I had met her or she would have known that she wasn't dealing with a feeble woman. Matter of fact, if she had done the research to get to know more about me, she would not have stuck her neck out as a martyr, because she would have known I was able to make it through a short term tough time.

This woman was confused by my makeup and fashion for a Barbie kind of girl, my age for not knowing much, and my situation as vulnerable. I was crazy as a bat to unveil myself to her which became the battle of Armageddon. She worked hard to make me out to be something that I was not and brought up hardships that were way too easy for me.

When I began working, she said, "Oh my, I

know that must be so hard for you." I looked at her with a smile and said, "No, not at all. I enjoy it and will be getting promoted very soon actually."

She knew in our trusted conversations that my husband and I weren't getting along, so I had begun to bring him with me. We showed great unity so it even made us stronger to block because she'd say, "How are things with your husband? It's pretty bad and I know some people who help families stay together because divorces hurt families."

This is another attempt whereby they always make a problem and then offer a solution so they can seem like a hero. I looked at her and with a big smile said, "Oh, is that for you? My husband and I are going out on a date tonight for some romance – we've been doing so good." It was true.

Don't worry too much about these people though, because they take their crazy with them everywhere they go. You aren't the only one who notices it. Just take the good that they give and don't allow their handicap to discourage you from continuing forward because they may bite you. In fact, this isn't even a person – it's a personality that I like to call Tara.

I have met several Taras on different jobs but none like the original. Once you Master a Tara, you are in the wisdom phase and can better discern your Compass.

Tara is the worst – she does things for no reason and doesn't realize it. Her ignorance is stronger than Paul Bunyan himself. And she is so friendly with everyone so it makes it hard for people to believe you. She also makes people beholding to her and even operates organizations that do great things for families so people in lesser circumstances are 'oh so grateful for her' and just adore what she does for the community.

But still, she is crazy and can't stay in one place too long before her mask starts itching to come off. That's why I say this whole thing is mapped out perfectly.

This may be the most difficult part of the book to comprehend so you may need to read it a few more times because it's also the most important. You have to know that the greater good is operating in your favor regardless of who is on your time.

Can you trust everyone? No! But you can trust God and how He will use them in your favor and towards his calling. All of their ways will build your muscle for future ones, so please do not pray them away or avoid them.

Seriously, do a separate study of psychology and get them down packed.

How do you view your calling in life from a Geographical view?

Do you have a clear View?

Who is in your Compass Now?

Are you prepared for opposition?

NOTE: Read the book of Proverbs. Most women pride themselves in being a Proverbs 31 woman, which is a fancy slogan. Instead, be the Entire book of Proverbs: stable, solid, and well-rounded.

Who is your Tara? This is how I created this Human Compass in the first place. I'm telling you, this is a beastly creature so strong it took me creating a team to get through it.

I had to Identify who was who in my life and wrote a short prelude of this book that I introduced to a professional PHD Psychologist, who highly recommended that I go forth with publishing it.

You will want to cuss this individual out, but they will sharpen you. Because they are looking for every little thing to criticize about you, you must clean every nook and cranny. I gave her nothing to talk about, held my tongue at the right moments, always appeared sharp, clean, and extremely positive with a good outlook on life.

I nailed it every time and I will say this – I was way sharper than she could keep up with – for someone to even criticize at all. But that's how these people are. They don't measure up to you, so they want to bring you beneath them. Don't even let them know that you see it. Follow the Compass and keep going.

CHAPTER 10
DIRECTION

Where are you going? The main thing is to have the answer to this question. In order to be consistent, you must be resilient and sure about where it is that you are going in life.

There is an old song that my family loved to sing called, "I'm coming up on the rough side of the mountain," by the Mighty Clouds of Joy.

In order to fully understand where you are going, you must identify where exactly you are coming from as well. Pinpoint your location and map out the road. What is the terrain? The obstacles? Know the land.

This is where study and research come into play of others who have gone before you. What mistakes did they make for you to avoid?

Many people read books about a person in magazines just to be like them. That's another thing. If you are going to read, make sure you do so the right way.

There is a book titled, *Think Like A Billionaire, Become A Billionaire* by Scot Anderson. These books are resources for you to take on the mindset, not how you actually become a Billionaire. It gives you an insight to the routine that a Billionaire has so that you can apply it to your own business. That's the major step in reading. To comprehend and apply otherwise, you have just looked at words... again.

When someone tells me they have read a book and their lifestyle does not reflect it, I am under the impression they cannot read, but are gifted in staring at words and flipping pages.

My professor in Programming Logic at college taught me how to read. As insulting as it was at first, it was much needed. I was reading the way I had always known how – skimming through the words that stood out to be the answer. One day I got stuck and told him that I didn't see what I was looking for. "Did you Read?" he said.

I responded, "Yes, I'm reading it now."

"No you are not; if you read the material, you wouldn't be asking that question. Now go back, sit down, and Read," he said.

I was thinking we don't have that much time in this class and I really want to get this done. I don't have time to sit here looking at every single last word and there is no telling where the answer is. I would have to reread the whole thing.

When I thought I found the answer, I performed it and my project did not turn out correctly. It looked 'right' to my eye, but it was actually wrong. He said, "It was supposed to be to the left."

When I looked at the chapter, I realized my eyes must have gotten weary along with my patience. He was right. I tried to explain myself, "Mr. Ed, I thought......."

That may be the last time I ever use that phrase in my life; he lit me up in the class room for saying that alone. His vocal volume was turned all the way up and intense. "THOUGHT? YOU THOUGHT? You had better KNOW!! Ms. Mac this goes to show that you are skimming and you can't do that here. Now READ."

I sat down and no matter how slow I was at

comprehending, I made sure that I did so. At the end of his lectures, he would ask the class, "Are there any questions?" and there was always a poor soul who put their hand in the air. He would say, "Did you READ, because if you read that wouldn't be a question."

I said Mr. Ed, "I have a question." By now I had run his patience thin.

"Before you even ask me, Ms. Mac, did you READ?"

"Yes sir, I've been reading you and I want to know what exactly is a good question."

Mr. Ed responded, "A Logic one because the answers to all others are in the literature. If you Read them carefully, you can apply it, but if you skim over something important, you will miss the very details that it takes in order for your program to run. One missing period or one missing comma can ruin your entire program. So READ."

There are no short cuts to your destination; it must be thoroughly researched. Reading books about a Billionaire teaches you their mindset. Reading biographies about them gives you stories that you can relate to of your own that can guide you. But if you really want to be a Billionaire, reading about Donald Trump isn't going to do it. Read about the field that he's in and apply it. Stocks and Trades.

Reading about Beyoncé won't do it. Read about the music industry, marketing, branding, and performance artist.

You have to Read a Map before you start in your direction. You can't just make it up as you go along because so many things that belong to the mission as it is will begin to fall into place and arise.

There is no time for you to begin trying to figure out what you should have already known in the first place. If you don't know where you're going, you wouldn't know if you were there or missed it.

Begin by identifying your current location.

✦ Where are you now?
✦ What do you need to have in order to get from A-Z?
✦ What tools will you use to get there?
✦ How long will it take? Create a deadline

+ What have been my obstacles and weaknesses in the past?
+ What are my strengths?
+ When do I plan to get started?
+ How can I keep it simple along the way so that I do not get distracted?

This is a big one. I have seen many people think they are already at their destination and begin to set up shop as if they were, just because they finally had the resources to do so. Don't confuse your financial success with your overall success.

If you planned to own a book publishing company on a national scale just because you wrote a best seller, it is no reason to sit and engage in the glory of that. Your feet should still be moving or you will be passed by someone else who understands the industry, wondering how come they reached your goal in such a short amount of time.

It's because they kept the victory dances short and kept moving to the next goal on the Map until they reached their destination – a classic 'turtle beats the hare' story – which happens more often than not. Did you READ?

CHAPTER 11

ACTIVATE

Now that we fully understand (comprehend) the Compass, it is time to Activate (Apply). This is the last step to Reading and the Return on your Investment (ROI).

Lay out your Map and identify where you are now.

Where are you going?

Surround yourself with people on the same mission as you.

Now... Identify those who are already in your Compass and who you need to add.

Work with them on a weekly basis near and far.

If they have material to read, do so. You don't have to reinvent the wheel.

Be Great!

WEBSITE AND CONTACT INFO:

www.facebook.com/Priscillamac/

Instagram: Priscilla Mac

Twitter: @prissymac1

Booking: priscillaprosperity@yahoo.com

www.ingramcontent.com/pod-product-compliance
Lightning Source LLC
Chambersburg PA
CBHW062056280526
45788CB00003B/1250